Behind the Scenes

TELEVISION

SARAH MEDINA

First published in 2009 by Wayland

Wayland
338 Euston Road
London NW1 3BH

Wayland Australia
Level 17/ 207 Kent Street
Sydney NSW 2000

Editor: Nicola Edwards
Design manager: Paul Cherrill
Designer: Rita Storey

British Library Cataloguing in Publication Data

Medina, Sarah, 1960-
TV. - (Behind the scenes)
1. Television - Vocational guidance - Juvenile literature
I. Title
791.4'5'0293

ISBN: 978 0 7502 5887 6

The author and publisher would like to thank the following for permission to reproduce the
following photographs in this book:
© Telepix/ Alamy p1, © Richard Naude/Alamy p5, © Alan Gignoux/Alamy p6, © David
Pearson/Alamy p7, © Stock Connection/Alamy p10, © Alan Hanson/Alamy p11, © Shoosmith
TV Collection Alamy p12, © pbpgalleries/Alamy p13, © Picture Contact/Alamy p14, © Keith
Morris/Alamy p15, © Adrian Buck Alamy p16 © Keith Morris/Alamy p19, © Adrian
Sherratt/Alamy p20, © Dan Atkin/Alamy p21, © Nicola Campbell/Alamy p22, © Michael
Dwyer/Alamy p23, © Justin Kase zsixz/Alamy pp 25 and 26, © Jacky Chapman/Alamy pp27
and 28, © Marwood Jenkins/Alamy p29;Vittorio Zunino Celotto/Getty Images p4, Courtney
Kealy/Getty Images p9, Valery Hache/AFP/Getty Images; istock p8 and 24: Shutterstock p17.
Cover image Valery Hache/AFP/Getty Images

Printed in China

Wayland is a division of Hachette Children's Books, an Hachette UK company.
www.hachette.co.uk

Contents

Introduction to television

Television, or TV, is a big part of modern-day life. Millions of people around the world own and watch a TV at home. People can watch TV programmes over the Internet and on mobile phones, too. In the UK, the average person spends about 25 per cent of his or her waking life watching TV!

Information and entertainment

People watch TV for news, information and entertainment. In schools and universities, educational programmes may be shown on TV. In business, people sometimes watch programmes for training and information purposes.

Broadcasters and indies

TV is part of the media industry. The TV industry is made up of a large number of broadcasters and production companies. The broadcasters are organizations that broadcast TV programmes to the public. The production companies,

↓ *The set of the Italian version of the television talent show 'The X Factor'. The rights to use the format of the programme have been sold to countries all over the world. Versions are now screened in countries as far apart as Australia, Colombia, Iceland and India.*

A TV crew on location in Newport, South Wales, filming an episode of 'Torchwood', a spin-off series from the hugely successful 'Dr Who', which is also filmed in Wales.

known as 'indies', are independent companies that often make TV programmes for broadcasters.

Broadcasters and indies often work closely together. Broadcasters may make some of their own TV programmes. Sometimes, a broadcaster buys in programmes from abroad, especially from the USA. But most TV programmes are made by an indie on a broadcaster's behalf. 'The X Factor', for example, is made for ITV by a super-indie called FremantleMedia.

Ideas for programmes may come from both broadcasters and indies. Indies invest a lot of time in developing new ideas. They take these ideas to broadcasters, in the hope that a broadcaster will commission them to make one or more of the programmes. Broadcasters may have great ideas, too, but they may not have a programme-making team.

Instead, they find the best indie to turn their idea into a programme they can broadcast on TV.

About this book

This book gives an overview of the television industry, and the key jobs within it. It includes first-hand accounts of people working in TV, and it will help you to work out whether working in TV is a good choice for you.

Any questions ?

Who are the main UK broadcasters?

In the UK, the BBC, ITV, Channel 4 and Five are all terrestrial broadcasters. There are about 300 cable and satellite broadcasters, including BSkyB, Virgin Media, Discovery and Disney.

Working in television

What do you think of when you think about working in TV? Often, the first things that come to mind are high-profile jobs such as acting or presenting. Actors and presenters are certainly part of the picture, but the TV industry has so much more to offer. Most jobs in TV are in four key areas: research and production, design, technical operations and post-production.

Research and production

Research and production is all about developing ideas and getting the programme-making process underway. Work in this area includes agreeing a concept, writing a first script and getting the programme-making team together. Budgets and schedules have to be worked out at an early stage, too. Some of the key jobs are: researcher, director, producer, production manager, floor manager and performer (see pages 8-13).

↑ Many people who work in TV, such as the actor and the make-up artist in this picture, are self-employed, and work may be irregular.

Any questions

Is it hard to get a job in TV?

Working in TV often seems glamorous, and this makes it a popular – and competitive – career choice. People in TV normally have to work really hard and be flexible to have a successful career. And, although some people in TV earn a lot of money, most do not; their choice is for an interesting job over a well-paid one.

Design

The area of design involves working on the 'look and feel' of a TV programme. For example, a drama series that is set in Victorian England needs to have sets, props and costumes that reflect that period. Performers need to wear suitable make-up and hairstyles. Some of the key design jobs are: set designer, costume designer, make-up artist, and graphic and visual effects design (see pages 14-17).

Technical operations

Technical operations is a term that covers all the technical processes involved in filming a TV programme. These include cameras, sound and lighting. They are all specialist areas, and each one is vital to a programme's success. Some of the key jobs in technical operations are: camera operators, script supervisors, sound recordists, electrical technicians and grips (see pages 18-21).

Post-production

Post-production is the area that brings everything together into a final programme after filming. During post-production, parts of a film may be cut and other parts pieced together. Visual effects and graphics are added, as well as different sounds, such as speech, music and sound effects. Some of the key jobs in post-production are: editor and re-recording mixer (see pages 22-23).

↓ *The TV industry needs staff with a wide range of skills, from creative ideas people to hands-on technical specialists – and everything in between!*

THINKING AHEAD

Two thirds of the people employed in the TV industry have a university degree. However, just as important – if not more so – as academic qualifications are qualities such as creativity and drive: having great ideas and the talent and energy to turn them into must-see TV programmes.

Research and production

Jobs in research and production are very varied, and different skills are needed for different jobs. Even within a particular role, people may be required to carry out a range of tasks. Flexibility and the ability to do several things at once are important.

Researcher

TV researchers work on the early stages of programme making. They often come up with new programme ideas. One of their main responsibilities is finding and checking out the facts and information that are needed to make a programme.

Research can be related to just about anything to do with the television programme, from the programme's content, to finding possible locations for filming and potential programme contributors, such as actors or presenters. Some research is relatively easy and quick, for example, reading through newspapers to find a suitable person to be interviewed on a news programme. Other research can take much longer – up to several months – for example, researching the historical background for a drama series.

←

Many researchers are able to work across different types of TV programme. Some of these programmes, such as those with medical or scientific content, need researchers who are specialists in their field.

Director

A director has overall creative responsibility for the way a TV programme is made. It is the director's vision and interpretation of an idea that we see when we watch our favourite programme on TV.

Most directors work in a particular area of TV programming, such as current affairs, comedy or drama. Studio directors work on programmes that are filmed in a studio. Location directors work in a variety of indoor and outdoor locations. Like many people in TV, directors often work on a freelance basis.

Directors work on a TV programme from beginning to end. They may be involved with commissioning new programmes. They read and interpret scripts, working out how to turn them into the best possible programme.

Directors are involved with many decisions, such as the programme design and filming locations, and approving the performers and crew. During filming, the whole team follows the director's instructions. During post-production, the director oversees and approves the final stages that make the completed programme ready to be shown.

↑ *The director of a morning television show talks to the programme's presenter during a dress rehearsal for the first broadcast. The programme is aired on a satellite TV station that aims its content specifically at Arab women in the Middle East.*

Producer

A producer's role can vary a lot, depending on the TV programme being made. On large-scale projects, there may be more than one producer. Like a director, a producer may be involved with many aspects of programme making. However, whereas a director has overall creative responsibility for a programme, a producer often has more hands-on, practical responsibility for the business side of the project.

Some producers, known as executive producers, come up with ideas for new programmes. They take these ideas to broadcasters who may decide to commission them. The executive producer may then be involved with checking scripts, or getting permission to turn a book into a TV programme.

On other programmes, producers may be more involved with the day-to-day details of making the programme. They may contribute to decisions about selecting the cast or the design of the set. Occasionally, some producers even do some directing!

Production manager

Production managers support the work of the producer. Their contribution helps to ensure that the production process runs smoothly, from beginning to end. To do this, they must work closely with the whole production team.

←

Producers need technical as well as managerial skills to help them oversee the production of a TV programme. Some producers specialize in a particular type of programme, such as quizzes, soaps or comedy shows.

A production manager's work often involves a lot of general administration and staff management. For example, production managers may write the contracts for production staff and performers. Another key job is looking after the schedule. They need to make sure that enough time is available for all the different aspects of filming. For example, they have to decide how many actors are needed on which days, and which locations are required on particular dates. They have to ensure that all deadlines are met.

THINKING AHEAD

A TV production manager needs to have a good understanding of the production process and finance. Because there is so much contact with people, it is important to have excellent communication skills, too.

It's my job!

Ellie: Producer

"What I love about my job is that every day is different. I make documentaries for a super-indie, and I've been able to travel all over the world and meet lots of different people. I have to stay on top of current affairs, which is really interesting. The downside can be all the meetings and the paperwork you have to get through!"

↓ Production managers need to have good financial skills, because part of their responsibility is looking after a programme's production budget.

Location manager

Location managers work closely with production managers on programmes that are filmed outdoors. They organize 'recces' (pronounced 'reckees'), which are visits to check out particular locations to see if they are suitable and available for filming. They agree contracts for using different locations, and they are in charge of the location during the shoot.

Floor manager

Floor managers work in a studio, and their role is to support the director during filming. Normally, a studio director gives instructions to performers and the crew by means of talkback communication. However, not everyone on the studio floor has headphones, and so the floor manager passes on any instructions that the director cannot give directly.

Performer

The term 'performer' covers many different people with many different skills! Some of the most visible and well-known performers on TV are actors and presenters. However, performers include many other kind of entertainers, such as singers, dancers, comedians and stunt performers. The type of performer required depends on the type of programme being made.

Performers normally work on a freelance basis, and are paid for each programme they are involved in. They have to attend meetings and auditions, in order to be selected for a job.

←

On location at Lake Windermere, a BBC TV crew films an episode of 'Street Doctor' with presenter Dr Ayan Panja.

Actor

An actor's job usually involves interpreting a script to bring characters to life. For some programmes, however, actors work without a script (called 'ad-libbing'). For example, the TV comedy 'Outnumbered' uses a combination of scripts and ad-libbing. As well as acting in TV programmes, actors may provide voice-overs for TV documentaries and adverts.

Presenter

Presenters introduce and host TV programmes, such as news, sports and music programmes, and game shows. Presenters may work in a studio or on location. Some presenters write their own scripts or interview questions. However, these may be written for them and, during filming, they read the script from an autocue. Sometimes, presenters are required to ad-lib.

Any questions ?

I'd like to be a TV presenter. How can I make that happen?

Many people think that being a television presenter sounds like an exciting and fun career so the competition to become one is fierce. You'll need bags of talent and confidence – and a lot of determination and perseverance, too. Start by studying your favourite presenters on TV: how do they control the programme by what they say and do, and how well can they ad-lib?

↓ Lewis Hamilton, the Formula 1 World Champion, gives an interview to TV sports presenter Steve Ryder. Presenters have to appear calm as they present their material and entertain the viewer – all while listening to detailed instructions from the director or floor manager!

Design

Jobs in design are all about developing and putting together the 'look and feel' of a TV programme. Design can be related to sets, to the clothes and make-up worn by performers or to graphics that form part of the finished programme.

Set designer

Set designers create the overall visual look of a TV programme, whether it is set in the present, the past or the future. Set designers are sometimes called production designers.

The script is the starting point for set design. Set designers study a script, so that they can come up with creative, fresh designs. They discuss and agree their ideas with the programme's director. Before filming, they oversee a team of people who build the set and decorate it with props. During rehearsals, set designers may make adjustments to the set.

Any questions

Who finds the props for a set?
Props staff are part of the design team for a TV programme. Part of their job is to find and provide smaller props, such as lampshades and vases, that make a programme seem realistic – and make it visually interesting. Props staff also help to build the set, ready for the shoot.

→ *The set design and props help to give each TV programme its own look and feel.*

Costume designer

Costume designers are sometimes known simply as 'wardrobe'. They design, hire and adapt costumes for TV programmes, so they need to be able to sew!

Depending on the programme, they may need to work on period, modern-day or futuristic designs. A costume designer has a big influence on the 'look and feel' of a TV programme. For historical drama programmes, for example, costume designers need to research and become very knowledgeable about the kinds of clothes that people wore in a particular period. This helps them to create costumes that are historically accurate, and which do not look out of place. They also need to understand the different characters in the programme, so they get a feel for how they would dress.

It's my job!

Kate: Costume designer

"I've just been appointed as a costume designer on a science fiction series for a major broadcaster. It's a great project, because I get to be pretty wild with my ideas! I have to work really closely with set and make-up design, too, and that's where planning meetings come in. It's great to do some preliminary research and then bounce ideas around with other design people."

⬇ *Members of the crew make last-minute adjustments to an actor's costume during the filming of a Welsh language TV drama.*

Make-up artist

Make-up artists are responsible for designing and applying the make-up for different TV performers before and during a shoot. They are also responsible for each performer's hairstyle, which may include designing wigs, hair extensions or bald caps. For some programmes, such as medical dramas, make-up artists may need to design and use prosthetics to create effects such as scars, cuts, bruises and the effects of illnesses.

Make-up for TV is very different from the make-up people wear in everyday life. During filming, the camera and lighting can be very unforgiving, for example, making wrinkles and skin blemishes look more obvious. Make-up artists need to make sure that these effects are counteracted. Before the shoot, a make-up artist may do test shots with camera operators to be sure that make-up and hair look good.

THINKING AHEAD

Make-up artists need to be creative and artistic. Understanding the fashion and styles of different periods and different people in society is important, so that they can recreate the right kind of look. Because they work so closely with performers, make-up artists need to be sociable – and sensitive to people's feelings.

← Make-up artists at work between takes. For this scene they have applied make-up to make the actor look older and have added bloodstains to his clothing to make it look as if he has been shot.

Graphic designers

Most TV programmes have an opening and closing sequence, showing the title of the programme and listing all the people who have been involved with its development. Graphic designers are responsible for creating these opening and closing sequences, as well as the other graphics, such as maps and diagrams, that are used in the TV programme.

↑ *Most graphics featured in TV programmes are generated by computer. This means that graphic designers working in television need to know their way around the various software programs used to create these graphics.*

Visual effects designers

Visual effects designers design and make a wide variety of special effects for TV programmes. Like graphic designers, visual effects designers use computer technology to create special effects, which can then be added to the programme in the post-production phase.

It's my job!

Rick: Visual effects designer

"I work for a small, independent visual effects company in London. I've just finished working on an effects sequence for a TV drama. We had to create some 3D animation and special effects, which were then combined with live action to reconstruct a plane crash. It's hard work, and very detailed – but it's fantastic to see your work in a finished programme, and to know that what you created brought something to life."

Technical operations

Cameras, sound and lighting are all part of technical operations. These three areas are all very specialized, and have to work together, and with the rest of the production team, to create a TV programme that reflects the director's vision.

Camera operator

A camera operator uses a combination of cameras and lighting equipment to film moving images for a TV programme. For some programmes, events are filmed as they happen and broadcast live. For others, the images are stored, so they can be edited and broadcast at a later date.

Camera operators often work as part of a team, called a camera crew. The head of the camera crew, called a senior lighting camera operator, studies the script and works closely with a programme's director, in order to plan the best way to film different scenes. Before the shoot, camera operators make sure that the cameras and other equipment are properly set up.

→ *Camera operators need to have good hand-eye coordination, to make sure that, for example, a scene in a drama or action in a sporting event is filmed accurately and in the best possible way.*

Camera operators need to have a through technical understanding of cameras and lighting equipment. At the same time, they need to be creative and have the ability to follow instructions and to work as part of a team.

→

In the TV industry, script supervisors are often known simply as 'continuity'. This member of the crew is taking notes as she watches and times each take. This will help the editing process to run smoothly later.

Script supervisor

Script supervisors work as part of the camera crew. Most TV programmes are filmed out of sequence; the end of a programme may be filmed before the beginning! Script supervisors are responsible for making sure that the programme eventually makes perfect sense, and that there is no break in continuity in any area.

Throughout the shoot, script supervisors take careful notes and keep detailed records of every single thing that is filmed at a particular time, including dialogue, action, costumes and props. This is the only way to ensure that nothing is missed or out of place when filming starts up again after a break.

It's my job!

Ed: Script supervisor

"To do this job, you have to be able to keep lots of things in your mind's eye at once. You have to be really organized; you rely a lot on the notes and records you make so, if they aren't thorough, you can get into problems. You need to be confident enough to make quick decisions, too. Sometimes, you have to stop a shoot if you can see a problem with continuity – for example, an actor wearing a pink shirt instead of a blue one when a scene has been shot over a couple of days!"

Sound recordist

Sound recordists are responsible for recording high-quality sound when a TV programme is filmed. They are sometimes known as production mixers. In order to do their job well, they need to be very familiar with the script and to work closely with the programme's director.

Sound recordists set up and operate sound recording equipment and other equipment, such as microphones, on a shoot. This may be in a studio or on location. Sound recording usually happens at the same time as filming. The quality of the sound is carefully monitored through a pair of headphones.

Sometimes, sound recordists record sound effects and music, and then play these into a live programme. In a studio, they may have to set up talkback communication between the director, the production team and performers.

THINKING AHEAD

First and foremost, sound recordists should have very sharp hearing and good concentration! Microphones are very sensitive and may pick up unwanted background sounds, such as cars passing on a nearby road; sound recordists need to be able to pick up these sounds, even though they may be very faint. The ability to use technical sound recording equipment is important, too.

← Sound operators give instructions to other sound staff, such as boom operators. Here, a boom operator is holding a boom microphone towards actors filming a scene in a television drama. The microphone has to be close to the actors, but not so close that it appears in the scene when it is shown on television!

Electrical technicians

Electrical technicians may be called lighting technicians, and they are often known as 'sparks', too. Electrical technicians are fully qualified electricians. They are responsible for the lighting equipment and for checking power supplies on a TV shoot.

Electrical technicians may be involved with creative decisions about lighting. Different lighting effects are needed, depending on whether the shoot is indoors or outdoors. By positioning lighting equipment in a particular way, and changing the strength of the light, electrical technicians can achieve different effects and help to achieve the director's vision for the programme.

↓ *An electrical technician takes a light reading before filming begins at a doctors' surgery which is being featured in a TV programme. As well as lighting outside broadcasts, electrical technicians have to set up lighting in TV studios in preparation for a shoot.*

Post-production

During post-production, the hard work of planning and filming a TV programme all comes together. The hope – and the plan – is that the finished programme matches the director's creative vision.

Editor

Editors are responsible for piecing together the final programme that viewers watch. To do this, they work in an editing suite on specialist equipment, where they can combine digital footage, speech, sound effects, music, graphics and visual effects.

During a shoot, much more material is filmed than is actually needed to make a programme of the correct length. Every piece of footage that is filmed is stored separately and has its own number. During editing, editors select the

THINKING AHEAD

Editors have a highly creative job. They need to be able to understand the brief the director gives them and to imagine the whole 'story' as they bring the programme together. Editors need to have strong technical ability, too, so they can use the specialist editing equipment. Editing is a detailed and time-consuming process, so patience is a must!

best footage for each scene. Using computer software, they join together the different pieces

← During editing, the aim is to achieve a programme that meets the director's requirements in terms of drama, impact and continuity.

of footage to form a sequence. All the sequences are then combined, and sound, music and visual effects added in, to make the programme that viewers will watch.

Although editors liaise closely with the director, they may work alone for a lot of the time during editing. On large projects, the editor may have an assistant editor to help with the editing process. The editor may also work with other post-production staff, such as re-recording mixers, who specialize in sound.

Re-recording mixer

Re-recording mixers are sometimes called dubbing mixers. Their job is to put together the final sound for a programme. To do this, they have to mix all the speech, sound effects and background music in the programme.

They may add extra sound effects at this stage, too. Sometimes, re-recording mixers edit speech to fit the action in the programme.

It's my job!

Adam: Re-recording mixer

"I work as a freelance re-recording mixer. When I'm on a job, I spend most my day in a sound-proofed studio or editing suite. It's important not to have any distractions — and to be able to concentrate! Not only do I have to listen carefully to the sound I'm working with, but I also have to focus to be able to handle all the complex sound equipment. When a programme's finished and I get to see - and hear - my contribution, it's really satisfying."

← Re-recording mixers need to have an excellent understanding of sound technology and equipment.

Being a runner

Runners are the most junior members of a TV production team. They are employed by some broadcasters and indies, often on a short-term basis. A runner may be asked to work in an office, recording studio or editing suite, or on location.

Any questions?

Why do people become runners?

Being a runner is a great way to get experience in the TV industry. By watching, learning, talking to people and being hands-on, runners can learn a great deal. This can help them when they apply for other, more permanent jobs. Runners can make good contacts, too. If they do a good job, people will often remember them. And, in such a competitive field, any small advantage can make a big difference.

Being a runner is hard work and not well-paid – and it is far from glamorous, too! It is more about running errands than about creating TV programmes or rubbing shoulders with famous people. Despite all this, many people jump at the chance to become a runner. In fact, being a runner is the most popular way to get a job in TV.

Runners should expect to be asked to do just about anything in their job. Although they normally report to a producer, director or editor, they may be asked to help out by just about anyone in the production team. Refreshments are frequently called for, for example!

→

Some of the individual tasks a runner has to do may not be very interesting, but being part of the whole programme-making process can be very exciting.

Basic office work, such as answering the phone, typing and photocopying, is a normal part of a runner's job. Running around delivering items such as scripts is also par for the course. Sometimes, runners may be asked to help out with basic research for a programme, as well as with tasks such as hiring props and checking paperwork. Having a driving licence is a good plus, because runners may be asked to transport the crew between filming locations.

THINKING AHEAD

Being a runner calls for lots of energy and enthusiasm rather than any particular training or qualifications. Being passionate about TV and willing to do whatever tasks are asked of them helps runners to get the best out of the experience. It is important to be a quick learner, cool under pressure and able to work independently.

↑ *Every day is different for a runner. On some days, they may be based in an office; on others, they may be out on location, such as here in Trafalgar Square, in the middle of London, with performers and the crew.*

Other jobs in television

Many of the jobs in TV are specialized. However, more general job opportunities are available, too. These include jobs in human resources (usually called HR), accounts, information technology (known as IT) and legal departments, and also in administration. Whatever their role, most people really enjoy being part of the TV industry.

Human resources

HR, or human resources, is all about human beings – the people who work for a broadcaster or indie. HR staff are involved with issues relating to staff employment, from hiring to firing. They can also advise employees who have work-related problems.

Accounts

Accounts staff are responsible for dealing with financial matters. They pay invoices – for hiring costumes or props for a shoot, for example. They receive payments too – for instance, from broadcasters from other countries who buy a particular programme. The accounts department is also responsible for staff pay, tax and pensions.

Information technology

The TV industry relies heavily on computers, from runners and other staff using office computers to editors working with complex editing software. IT staff help to set up IT equipment. Most people who work in TV are capable computer users, but when things go wrong, IT help staff are also essential to get people up and running again quickly.

→

Doing work experience in a TV company is a great way to get a behind-the-scenes view of the different areas of the television industry.

Legal

Legal staff give advice to other staff in TV on a range of issues. For example, they may help HR staff with queries about employment law, or they may advise a researcher or director on whether or not information to be included in a programme is libellous.

Legal staff may also draw up contracts for people who are involved in a programme, many of whom work on a freelance basis. Legal staff who work for a broadcaster or an indie are normally qualified lawyers.

↓ *There is a saying in TV that 'You are only as good as your last job' so, whatever work you do, you need to make it your very best!*

Administration

Many jobs in TV need administration (often called 'admin') support. The administrators do tasks that support other staff, such as typing letters and reports, photocopying and filing.

Any questions?

How do I get into TV?

TV jobs are in high demand and, often, people need a university degree to get a foot in the door. However, there are other ways in to the industry. Doing work experience, or working as a runner, gives you experience and contacts that can lead to the job you really want.

Television and you

TV is one of the most creative industries there is. Being involved in making a TV programme and seeing 'your' programme on TV, knowing that people enjoy it and hearing them talk about it, is incredibly satisfying.

At the same time, working in TV can be very stressful. People often work under a lot of pressure, with tight schedules and budgets. The hours can be long, and conditions, especially on an outdoor shoot, may be hard. Despite its glamorous image, the day-to-day reality of working in TV may be quite the opposite!

If you are interested in working in TV, it helps to find out as much as you can about the industry. Reading this book is a good start! You will be able to find out more information from a careers office or library. The further information list on page 31 will point you in the direction of some useful books and websites.

↓ *A decorator works on the interior of a set for a TV programme to be filmed in Salford, England. There is always a place in TV for people who are skilled in a particular craft, such as carpentry, and painting and decorating.*

Students on a university media course. Some are learning presenting skills in front of the camera, while others are gaining experience of using sound, lighting and camera equipment.

Think about the kinds of interests you have, and what you are good at. Do these tie in with a particular job or area in TV? For example:

- Do you enjoy digging out information? If so, you could consider becoming a researcher.

- Are you into fashion – not just what's in right now, but what people have worn over history? In that case, costume design might be for you.

- Are you patient and happy to concentrate for long periods of time? You could consider being an editor.

Research the qualities and skills you need to work in the area of TV that interests you. For example, to be a script supervisor, you need to have an excellent memory, and you have to be calm and highly organized. These are qualities;

they are largely to do with your personality. You also need to understand the TV production process. This is a skill, and it can be learned.

If TV is for you, then research, plan and prepare. It is a competitive world, but it is very rewarding. Do everything you can to achieve your goal. Good luck!

Any questions

Can I study TV?

Some universities and film schools offer media courses, which give people an overview of the TV industry, as well as more practical training. However, they are not essential to work in TV. With a real passion for TV, and lots of persistence and hard work, it is possible to get that all-important first job.

Glossary

audition a short performance given by a performer to show their suitability for a programme

autocue a device that allows presenters to read text whilst looking at the TV camera

broadcast to send out a programme on TV

broadcaster an organization that broadcasts TV programmes to the public

budget money allocated to a project

cable when TV channels are broadcast using wires under the ground

commission to choose someone to do a piece of work, and tell them what is needed

concept an idea for a programme or series

contract a legal agreement, for example, between a TV channel and a TV company that makes a series of programmes for broadcast

crew a group of people who work together

digital footage a piece of film that is shot using a digital camera (that is, a type of camera that records images that can be viewed on a computer)

edit to prepare a final programme by deciding what will be included and removing any mistakes

employment law the legal rules relating to people who work for a company or an organization

freelance someone who is self-employed and who works for a company on a project-by-project basis

graphics visual material used as part of a TV programme

libellous containing false information about a person

media newspapers, TV and radio

production company a company that makes TV programmes; also called an indie

prop an object featured on a set, such as a lamp or vase, to make the set seem natural and realistic

prosthetics appliances made of materials such as rubber, plastic or silicone, which are attached to an actor's face or body to change its shape or appearance

satellite when TV channels are broadcast using satellites in space

schedule list of activities to be completed on a project, with dates by which each activity needs to be completed

script a document with the words that will be spoken during a programme

self-employed when people work for themselves or have their own business, rather than working for an employer

set the collection of scenery that is used for a scene in a programme

shoot the filming of a particular scene for a programme

sound effect a sound other than speech or music, which is added to a programme to make it seem more realistic or to create a special effect

super-indie a large independent production company that may employ thousands of people across the world

studio a room with specialist equipment where a programme is filmed

talkback communication a system of two-way communication

terrestrial when TV channels are broadcast from stations on the ground and do not use satellites

voice-over words spoken by a person that cannot be seen

work experience a short period of time that someone spends working for a television company, often without pay

Further information

The Creative and Media Diploma

The Diploma is a qualification for 14 to 19 year-olds which combines classroom-based study with practical hands-on work experience. It enables you to find out more about the careers you're interested in without having to commit to one of them. Find out more information about the Creative and Media Diploma at:
http://yp.direct.gov.uk/diplomas/subjects/Creative_Media/index.cfm

TV Qualifications and Training

Most people who work in TV go to university from school. Many do a media studies degree, but this is not essential for all jobs in TV. Opportunities are always available for people who show talent and dedication, even if they have not taken a media-specific course.

Books

How to Get A Job in Television by Susan Walls, How To Books Ltd, 2005

How to Get a Job in Television: Build Your Career from Runner to Series Producer by Elsa Sharp, Methuen Drama, 2009

Websites

For general information and advice about careers, see:
www.connexions-direct.com/index.cfm?go=Careers

For information on work experience prospects look at:
http://www.prospects.ac.uk/cms/ShowPage/Home_page/Explore_types_of_jobs/Types_of_Job/p!eipaL?state=showocc&idno=462&pageno=3

For information about working in the TV industry, and relevant training courses, visit these websites:
www.skillset.org/tv

www.prospects.ac.uk/cms/ShowPage/Home_page/Explore_job_sectors/Broadcast__film_and_interactive_media/overview/p!eigLac

http://www.startintv.com/resources/whichtvjobforme.php

For information on getting started in the entertainment industry go to:
http://www.thestage.co.uk/connect/howto/

You can read a director's diary of the making of a TV film on location at:
http://www.bbc.co.uk/history/programmes/timewatch/diary_pol_04.shtml

Index

Numbers in **bold** refer to pictures.

Behind the Scenes

Contents of titles in the series:

WAYLAND